The best meditation for women

DISCOVERING INNER PEACE, STRENGTH, AND WISDOM.

MEDITATION SERIES

MANON DOUCET

EDITED BY LAURIE DOUCET

EDITED BY JENNIFER GERMANO

ILLUSTRATED BY MANON DOUCET

To my book writers group, whose unwavering support and encouragement kept me inspired throughout the writing process of this book. Your feedback and insights were invaluable.

To my daughter Laurie, whose strength, resilience, and love continue to inspire me every day. I dedicate this book to you with gratitude for being my greatest teacher.

To my partner Andre, whose unwavering love, patience, and support allowed me to dive deep into my practice and bring forth this offering.

Thanks.

"Within every woman, there is a wild and natural creature, a powerful force, filled with good instincts, passionate creativity, and ageless knowing. Her name is Woman, and she belongs to the Moon."

Clarissa Pinkola Estés, Women Who Run With the Wolves.

Introduction

* * *

Welcome to "Best Meditation for Women" a book that will take you on a journey of self-discovery and empowerment through daily meditations. In these pages, you will find practical and accessible meditations designed specifically for women to help you cultivate inner peace, strength, and wisdom. Meditation is a powerful tool that can help reduce stress, anxiety, and negative emotions while improving focus, clarity, and overall well-being. With this book, you will learn how to integrate meditation.

CHAPTER 1
The Best Meditations for Women

* * *

Welcome to **"The Best Meditations for Women,"** a book that is designed to help women tap into their inner strength and wisdom through daily meditation practices. This book is a guide for women who are looking for ways to cultivate more peace, balance, and joy in their lives.

As a woman, you may have many responsibilities and demands on your time, leaving you feeling overwhelmed and stressed. The good news is that meditation can help you manage these feelings and find a sense of calm amidst the chaos. By taking just a few minutes each day to meditate, you can cultivate a deeper sense of inner peace and harmony that will help you navigate life's challenges with greater ease and grace.

The meditations in this book are specifically designed for women and are intended to help you connect with your inner wisdom, intuition, and creativity. They are designed to help you cultivate a greater sense of self-awareness and self-love, which are essential components of living a fulfilling and meaningful life.

Throughout the pages of this book, you will find meditations that are both practical and accessible. Each meditation is designed to be completed in just a few minutes a day, making it easy to fit into even the busiest of schedules. You don't need any prior experience with meditation to benefit from the practices in this book. All you need is an open mind and a willingness to try something new.

As you work your way through the meditations in this book, you will notice a shift in your energy and perspective. You may find that you feel more centered and grounded, more connected to your inner self and the world around you. You may also notice that your stress levels decrease, your focus improves, and your overall sense of well-being is enhanced.

The meditations in this book are accompanied by quotes and food for thought that are designed to inspire and uplift you. Each day, you will have the opportunity to reflect on your experience and write in your journal, deepening your connection with yourself and your inner wisdom.

As the author of this book, I am passionate about helping women cultivate a greater sense of inner peace and strength through meditation. I have seen firsthand how meditation can transform lives, and I am excited to share this practice with you. My hope is that this book will serve as a valuable tool on your journey toward greater well-being, joy, and fulfillment.

. . .

So, take a deep breath, and let's begin. Together, we will explore the best meditations for women, and discover the power of meditation to transform your life from the inside out.

Personal notes:

* * *

- _____
- _____
- _____
- _____
- _____
- _____
- _____
- _____
- _____
- _____
- _____
- _____
- _____
- _____
- _____
- _____

CHAPTER 2

The Power of Meditation

* * *

Meditation is a way of listening to your heart and soul, connecting with your inner self, and accessing your deepest wisdom. By taking a few minutes each day to meditate, you can quiet your mind, release tension, and cultivate a sense of inner peace. As you deepen your meditation practice, you may also find that you gain clarity, insight, and a heightened sense of intuition.

Meditation is a powerful tool that can help you tap into your innermost being and unlock your full potential. When we meditate, we create a space of stillness and quiet within ourselves. This space allows us to become more aware of our thoughts, feelings, and emotions without becoming overwhelmed by them.

Through meditation, we can learn to observe our thoughts without judgment, which can be incredibly liberating. We can begin to see our thoughts as passing clouds, coming and going, rather than as fixed, unchanging realities. This perspective can help us let go of negative thoughts, emotions and cultivate a sense of inner peace and well-being.

In addition to calming the mind, meditation can also have a positive impact on our physical health. Studies have shown that meditation can lower blood pressure, reduce stress and anxiety, and improve sleep quality.

Ultimately, meditation is a way of connecting with our deepest selves and with the world around us. By taking a few moments each day to meditate, we can access a wellspring of inner wisdom and strength and cultivate a deeper sense of purpose and meaning in our lives.

Meditation is a powerful tool for cultivating inner peace, reducing stress, and connecting with our inner wisdom. As such, I encourage you to make meditation a daily practice. Whether you have five minutes or an hour, take the time to sit in stillness and connect with your breath and your inner self.

As you embark on your daily meditation practice, I encourage you to reflect on the quote of the day. Each quote is carefully chosen to inspire and uplift and to help you connect with your inner wisdom. Use the quote as a point of focus during your meditation practice, and allow it to guide you toward greater peace and clarity.

In addition to the quote, I invite you to reflect on the food for thought of the day. This may be a question to ponder, a prompt for journaling, or a suggestion for mindfulness practice. Use this as an opportunity to deepen your awareness and understanding of yourself and to cultivate a greater sense of compassion and understanding.

Finally, I encourage you to take the time to write in your journal each day. Reflect on your experiences during your meditation practice, and explore your thoughts and feelings in more depth. Use your journal as a tool for self-discovery and growth, and allow it to be a source of support and inspiration on your journey towards greater peace and well-being.

Personal notes:

* * *

- _____
- _____
- _____
- _____
- _____
- _____
- _____
- _____
- _____
- _____
- _____
- _____
- _____
- _____
- _____
- _____
- _____

CHAPTER 3
The Daily Meditations

* * *

Each day, we will explore a different meditation designed to help you connect with your inner self and enhance your overall well-being. Here are a few examples:

Day 1: Let Go of Worry
"Let go of worry and trust that everything will work out." This meditation encourages you to release your fears and trust in the universe to guide you.

* * *

Day 2: Body Scan Meditation
This meditation involves scanning your body from head to toe, noticing any areas of tension or discomfort, and sending them loving-kindness.

* * *

Day 3: Loving-Kindness Meditation
This meditation involves sending love and kindness to yourself, your loved ones, and even those who challenge you.

* * *

Day 4: Gratitude Meditation
This meditation involves focusing on the things you are grateful for in your life.

* * *

Day 5: Forgiveness Meditation
This meditation involves cultivating forgiveness towards yourself and others.

* * *

Day 6: Visualization Meditation
This meditation involves visualizing a peaceful and serene place, such as a beach or forest.

* * *

Day 7: Silent Meditation
This meditation involves sitting in silence and observing your thoughts without judgment.

* * *

DAY 1: LET GO OF WORRY

"Let go of worry and trust that everything will work out."

Today's meditation is focused on letting go of worry and cultivating trust in the universe. Many of us spend a lot of time worrying about the future, but the truth is that worry does not change anything. It only causes unnecessary stress and anxiety. Instead, try to release your fears and trust that everything will work out as it should.

Begin by finding a quiet place to sit comfortably. Take a few deep breaths, and with each exhale, release any tension or worry that you may be holding in your body. When you feel relaxed and centered, begin to repeat the following mantra to yourself: "I release my worries and trust that everything will work out as it should."

As you repeat this mantra, try to visualize yourself releasing your fears and allowing the universe to guide you. Imagine that you are floating on a gentle stream, being carried effortlessly toward your destination.

If you find that your mind starts to wander, simply bring your attention back to the mantra and the visualization. Repeat this meditation for a few minutes or for as long as you feel comfortable.

Food for Thought:
When we worry, we are living in a future that hasn't happened yet. By letting go of worry, we can live in the present moment and trust that everything will work out as it should.

. . .

Journal Lines: What worries am I holding onto that I can release? How can I cultivate trust in the universe?

_____
_____
_____
_____
_____
_____
_____
_____
_____
_____
_____
_____

DAY 2: BODY SCAN MEDITATION

"Your body is your temple. Keep it pure and clean for the soul to reside in." - B.K.S Iyengar.

Today's meditation is focused on the body scan technique. It is a powerful way to cultivate self-awareness and release tension in the body. By paying attention to our body, we can learn to listen to its needs and promote healing and well-being.

Begin by finding a comfortable position, either sitting or lying down. Close your eyes and take a few deep breaths, allowing your body to relax. Once you feel calm and centered, begin to scan your body from head to toe, noticing any areas of tension or discomfort.

. . .

As you scan your body, send loving-kindness to each area that you identify. For example, if you notice tension in your shoulders, visualize sending love and kindness to that area. Imagine that you are wrapping that area in a warm, comforting blanket.

If you find that your mind starts to wander, simply bring your attention back to the body scan and the loving-kindness practice. Repeat this meditation for a few minutes or for as long as you feel comfortable.

Food for Thought:
Our bodies are our homes, and we must take care of them. By practicing the body scan meditation, we can learn to listen to our body's needs and promote healing and well-being.

Journal Line:
What areas of my body are holding tension or discomfort? How can I show loving-kindness to my body today?

_____
_____
_____
_____
_____
_____
_____
_____

_____
_____
_____
_____
_____
_____
_____
_____
_____
_____
_____
_____
_____
_____

DAY 3: LOVING-KINDNESS MEDITATION

"The love and attention you always wanted from someone else, is the love and attention you first need to give to yourself." - Bryant McGill

Today's meditation is focused on cultivating love and kindness towards ourselves and others. By sending love and kindness to those around us, we can create positive energy and connections in our lives.

Begin by finding a comfortable position and taking a few deep breaths, allowing your body to relax. Once you feel calm and centered, begin to visualize yourself in your mind's eye. See yourself surrounded by a warm, loving light. Repeat the following phrases to yourself:

> **"May I be happy.**
> **May I be healthy.**
> **May I be at peace."**

After a few minutes, visualize a loved one in your mind's eye. See them surrounded by a warm, loving light. Repeat the following phrases to them:

> **"May you be happy.**
> **May you be healthy.**
> **May you be at peace."**

Next, visualize someone who challenges you, such as a difficult coworker or family member. See them surrounded by a warm, loving light. Repeat the following phrases to them:

> **"May you be happy.**
> **May you be healthy.**
> **May you be at peace."**

If you find that your mind starts to wander, simply bring your attention back to the loving-kindness phrases and the visualization practice. Repeat this meditation for a few minutes or for as long as you feel comfortable.

Food for Thought:

By sending love and kindness to ourselves and others, we can create positive energy and connections in our lives. It all starts with cultivating love and kindness within ourselves.

Journal Line:
How can I show more love and kindness to myself and those around me? What positive changes might result from cultivating more love and kindness in my life?

_____
_____
_____
_____
_____
_____
_____
_____
_____

DAY 4: GRATITUDE MEDITATION

"Gratitude unlocks the fullness of life. It turns what we have into enough, and more. It turns denial into acceptance, chaos into order, and confusion into clarity. It can turn a meal into a feast, a house into a home, a stranger into a friend." - Melody Beattie.

Today's meditation is focused on cultivating a sense of gratitude for the abundance in our lives. By focusing on what we are grateful for, we can shift our perspective to one of positivity and abundance.

. . .

Begin by finding a comfortable position and taking a few deep breaths, allowing your body to relax. Once you feel calm and centered, begin to focus on something in your life that you are grateful for. It could be something as simple as a sunny day or the laughter of a loved one. Hold this thought in your mind, and repeat the following phrase to yourself:

"I am grateful for this moment of abundance."

As you focus on this thought, allow yourself to feel the warmth and joy that comes with gratitude. Take a few deep breaths and allow yourself to bask in this feeling of abundance.

Next, shift your focus to something else in your life that you are grateful for, and repeat the phrase:

"I am grateful for this moment of abundance."

Continue this practice for a few minutes, focusing on different things in your life that bring you joy and abundance.

Food for Thought:
By focusing on what we are grateful for, we can shift our perspective to one of positivity and abundance. What are some things in your life that you are grateful for? How can you cultivate a sense of gratitude in your daily life?

Journal Line:
Write down three things you are grateful for today. How do these things bring abundance and positivity into your life?

DAY 5: FORGIVENESS MEDITATION

"To forgive is to set a prisoner free and discover that the prisoner was you." - Lewis B. Smedes.

Today's meditation is focused on cultivating forgiveness towards yourself and others. By releasing the burden of anger and resentment, we can experience a sense of freedom and peace.

Begin by finding a comfortable position and taking a few deep breaths, allowing your body to relax. Once you feel calm and centered, bring to mind a person or situation that has caused you pain or hurt. Allow yourself to feel the emotions that come with this memory, but do not dwell on them. Instead, focus on releasing any feelings of anger or resentment towards this person or situation.

Repeat the following phrase to yourself:

> **"I release my anger and resentment towards [name of person/situation]. I forgive them, and I forgive myself."**

As you focus on this phrase, allow yourself to feel a sense of release and freedom. Take a few deep breaths and allow yourself to bask in this feeling of forgiveness.

Next, focus on yourself and any feelings of anger or resentment you may be holding towards yourself. Repeat the following phrase:

> **"I release my anger and resentment towards myself. I forgive myself for any mistakes or shortcomings."**

Continue this practice for a few minutes, focusing on forgiveness towards yourself and others.

Food for Thought:
Forgiveness is a powerful tool for releasing pain and hurt. Who do you need to forgive in your life? How can you cultivate a sense of forgiveness towards yourself and others?

Journal Line:
Write down the names of three people or situations that you need to forgive. How can you begin the process of forgiveness in your life?

DAY 6: VISUALIZATION MEDITATION

"Visualize your highest self, and start showing up as her." This meditation involves visualizing a peaceful and serene place, such as a beach or forest. Visualization can help calm the mind and reduce stress, as well as strengthen the connection between the mind and body.

To begin this meditation, find a quiet and comfortable place to sit or lie down. Close your eyes and take a few deep breaths. Imagine yourself in a peaceful place, such as a beach, forest, or mountaintop. Allow yourself to fully immerse in the experience by using all of your senses. What do you see, hear, feel, smell, and taste? Allow yourself to feel fully present in this space, and let any stress or worries melt away.

. . .

Food for Thought:
Visualization can be a powerful tool for manifesting your goals and desires. By visualizing your ideal self and life, you can start to attract these things into your reality. What are some things you would like to manifest in your life? How can visualization help you achieve these goals?

Journal Line:
Write about your visualization experience. What did you imagine? How did it make you feel? Did you notice any changes in your mood or mindset after the meditation?

_____
_____
_____
_____
_____
_____
_____
_____
_____
_____
_____
_____
_____
_____

DAY 7: SILENT MEDITATION

"Silence is a source of great strength." This meditation involves sitting in silence and observing your thoughts without judgment. This type of meditation can help increase self-awareness and reduce stress and anxiety.

. . .

To begin this meditation, find a quiet and comfortable place to sit. Close your eyes and take a few deep breaths. Allow your mind to settle into a state of stillness. Observe any thoughts or sensations that arise without judgment. If your mind begins to wander, gently bring your attention back to your breath.

Food for Thought:

Silence can be uncomfortable for many people, as it can bring up feelings of anxiety or restlessness. However, it is important to remember that these feelings are temporary and will pass. How can you cultivate a sense of peace and stillness in your daily life, even when things are chaotic or busy?

Journal Line:

Write about your experience with silent meditation. Was it challenging to sit in silence? Did you notice any recurring thoughts or patterns? How can you use this practice to cultivate more self-awareness and presence in your daily life?

_____
_____
_____
_____
_____
_____
_____
_____
_____
_____

MANON DOUCET

Personal notes:

* * *

- _____
- _____
- _____
- _____
- _____
- _____
- _____
- _____
- _____
- _____
- _____
- _____
- _____
- _____
- _____
- _____
- _____
- _____

CHAPTER 4
The Journey Continues

* * *

As you continue to practice these daily meditations, you will find that your sense of inner peace and well-being deepens. You may also notice that you feel more centered, grounded, and connected to your inner self. Remember that meditation is a journey, and each day is an opportunity to deepen your practice and connect with your inner wisdom.

In addition to deepening your sense of peace and well-being, regular meditation can bring many other benefits to your life. For example, it can help you manage stress and anxiety, improve your sleep, boost your immune system, and even lower your blood pressure.

As you continue your meditation practice, you may also find that you begin to experience moments of insight and clarity. You may gain a deeper understanding of yourself and your relationships, and begin to see the world in a new and more compassionate way.

One helpful mindfulness phrase to keep in mind as you meditate is "let go." When you notice your mind becoming distracted or caught up in thoughts or emotions, simply let them go and return your attention to your breath or the present moment.

Another helpful phrase is "This too shall pass." This can be a comforting reminder during times of stress or difficulty that the present moment, no matter how challenging, will eventually pass.

As you journey deeper into your meditation practice, remember to be gentle and patient with yourself. Meditation is not about achieving perfection or forcing your mind to be still. Rather, it is about cultivating a sense of presence, awareness, and compassion toward yourself and others.

Quote for the day:

"Meditation is not a way of making your mind quiet. It is a way of entering into the quiet that is already there - buried under the 50,000 thoughts the average person thinks every day." - Deepak Chopra.

Journal Line:
Take a moment to reflect on the benefits you have experienced from your meditation practice so far. What have you noticed about your thoughts, emotions, and overall well-being?

_____
_____
_____
_____

Personal notes:

* * *

- _____
- _____
- _____
- _____
- _____
- _____
- _____
- _____
- _____
- _____
- _____
- _____
- _____
- _____
- _____
- _____
- _____

CHAPTER 5
7-Days Meditation Challenge

* * *

In this chapter, we invite you to take a 7-day meditation challenge. Each day, we will explore a different meditation designed to help you deepen your connection with your inner self and cultivate a sense of inner peace.

- **Day 1: Mindful Breathing Meditation**
- **Day 2: Body Scan Meditation**
- **Day 3: Loving-Kindness Meditation**
- **Day 4: Gratitude Meditation**
- **Day 5: Forgiveness Meditation**
- **Day 6: Visualization Meditation**
- **Day 7: Silent Meditation**

WELCOME TO DAY 1 OF THE 7-DAY MEDITATION CHALLENGE!

Are you ready to dive deeper into your meditation practice and experience a greater sense of peace and calm? Today, we will start with a foundational meditation technique that can help you stay present and focused - the Mindful Breathing Meditation.

Sit in a comfortable position, close your eyes, and begin to focus on your breath. Pay attention to the sensation of the breath moving in and out of your body. If your mind wanders, simply bring your attention back to your breath. You can count your breaths, focusing on the count and taking slow, deep breaths.

Quote for the day:

"The present moment is the only time that is truly alive." - Thich Nhat Hanh.

Food for thought:

How often do you find yourself lost in thoughts about the past or future, neglecting the present moment? By practicing mindfulness and focusing on the breath, we can train our minds to be more present and aware.

Journal line:

What did you notice during your mindful breathing meditation today? How did it make you feel? Write down any thoughts or emotions that come up.

_____
_____
_____
_____

_____
_____
_____
_____
_____
_____

WELCOME TO DAY 2 OF YOUR 7-DAY MEDITATION CHALLENGE!

Today, we will explore the powerful practice of body scan meditation. This practice involves scanning your body from head to toe, noticing any areas of tension or discomfort, and sending them loving-kindness.

As you settle into a comfortable position, take a few deep breaths and focus your attention on your body. Begin at the top of your head and slowly scan down to your toes. As you move through each part of your body, take note of any areas of discomfort or tension, and imagine sending them love and kindness. You can use phrases such as "May my body be filled with ease" or "May I be kind to my body" as you scan.

Remember that the goal of body scan meditation is not to change or fix anything in your body, but simply to become aware and offer kindness. With each scan, you may find that your body begins to relax and release any tension or stress.

Quote of the day:

"The body is a vehicle for the mind, and meditation is the fuel." - Unknown.

Food for thought:
How often do you truly pay attention to your body and its sensations? Can you approach your body with love and kindness, even in moments of discomfort?

Journal line:
Take a few moments to write down any insights or observations from your body scan meditation practice. How did it feel to focus on your body in this way?

_____
_____
_____
_____

WELCOME TO DAY 3 OF THE 7-DAY MEDITATION CHALLENGE!

Today, we will be practicing the powerful Loving-Kindness Meditation. This meditation is all about cultivating love and kindness towards yourself and others.

Are you ready to open your heart and experience the beauty of love and kindness? Let's begin.

Exercise:

- **Find a comfortable seated position with your eyes closed.**

- Take a few deep breaths and allow your mind and body to relax.
- Begin by bringing to mind someone in your life who you love and care for deeply. It could be a family member, friend, or even a pet.

Visualize this person in your mind's eye and silently repeat the following phrases to yourself:

May you be happy
May you be healthy
May you be safe
May you be peaceful

Repeat these phrases for a few minutes before moving on to the next person.

- Next, bring to mind someone who you have difficulty with, someone who challenges you, or someone who you have negative feelings towards.
- Repeat the same phrases for this person, sending them love and kindness.

Finally, turn your attention towards yourself and repeat the phrases:

May I be happy
May I be healthy
May I be safe
May I be peaceful

- Sit for a few moments in silence, breathing deeply and feeling the love and kindness you have cultivated within yourself.

Quote for the day:

"Love and kindness are never wasted. They always make a difference. They bless the one who receives them, and they bless you, the giver." - Barbara De Angelis.

Food for thought:

How would your life be different if you approached every situation with love and kindness?

Journal line:

Write about a time when you received love and kindness from someone unexpected. How did it make you feel? How can you pay it forward to others?

_____
_____
_____
_____
_____
_____
_____
_____
_____
_____
_____
_____
_____
_____
_____
_____

_____

_____

_____

_____

_____

_____

WELCOME TO DAY 4 OF OUR 7-DAY MEDITATION CHALLENGE!

Today, we will be focusing on gratitude meditation, which is a powerful practice to cultivate feelings of appreciation and thankfulness for the present moment. By taking time to reflect on the good in your life, you can shift your mindset to one of abundance and positivity.

Exercise:

1. Find a comfortable seated position and close your eyes.
2. Take a few deep breaths and bring to mind someone or something that you are grateful for.
3. Hold this person or thing in your mind and reflect on why you are grateful for them.
4. Imagine sending them a wave of love and appreciation, feeling it radiate from your heart and fill your entire body.
5. Repeat this process, focusing on different people or things that you are grateful for, and allowing yourself to fully feel the gratitude and appreciation.

Quote for the day:

"Gratitude turns what we have into enough and more. It turns denial into acceptance, chaos into order, confusion into clarity...it makes sense of our past, brings peace for today, and creates a vision for tomorrow." - Melody Beattie.

Food for thought:
Take a moment to reflect on what you are grateful for today. It can be something as small as a warm cup of coffee or as big as a promotion at work. Write down at least three things you are grateful for and savor the positive emotions that come with acknowledging them.

Journal line:
Write about a time when you felt immense gratitude in your life. How did it feel to experience that emotion? How can you cultivate more gratitude in your daily life?

_____
_____
_____
_____
_____
_____
_____
_____
_____
_____
_____
_____
_____
_____

_____

_____

_____

_____

WELCOME TO DAY 5 OF OUR MEDITATION CHALLENGE!

Today, we will focus on the powerful practice of forgiveness meditation. Forgiveness is a crucial step in the healing process, as it allows us to let go of anger, resentment, and negative feelings toward ourselves and others. By cultivating forgiveness, we open ourselves up to greater compassion, love, and inner peace.

Exercise:

1. Find a quiet place where you can sit comfortably and be undisturbed for 10-15 minutes.
2. Close your eyes and take a few deep breaths to center yourself.
3. Bring to mind someone you have been holding a grudge against or resenting. It could be yourself, a friend, a family member, a coworker, or anyone else.
4. Imagine them in front of you and repeat the following phrases silently to yourself: "I forgive you. Please forgive me. Let us both be free."
5. Allow yourself to feel any emotions that arise and continue repeating the phrases for as long as you need to.

Quote of the day:

"Forgiveness is not always easy. At times, it feels more painful than the wound we suffered to forgive the one that inflicted it. And yet, there is no peace without forgiveness." - Marianne Williamson.

Food for thought:

Reflect on a time when someone forgave you, and how that made you feel. What would it feel like to offer that same sense of forgiveness to someone else?

Journal line:

Write about a situation in your life where you feel stuck or resentful. Can you identify any opportunities for forgiveness? How might cultivating forgiveness help you move forward?

_____
_____
_____
_____
_____
_____
_____
_____
_____
_____
_____
_____
_____
_____
_____
_____
_____
_____

_____
_____
_____
_____

* * *

WELCOME TO DAY 6 OF THE 7-DAY MEDITATION CHALLENGE!

Are you ready to dive deeper into your inner world? Today, we will be exploring visualization meditation, a powerful tool for manifesting your deepest desires and tapping into your creative potential.

Visualization meditation is all about using your imagination to create vivid mental images of the reality you want to experience. It's a fun and exciting practice that can help you break free from limiting beliefs and tap into your full potential.

To begin, find a quiet and comfortable place to sit. Close your eyes and take a few deep breaths. When you're ready, visualize a scenario in your mind that represents your desired outcome. This can be anything, from a successful career to a happy relationship or a peaceful home.

Once you have a clear picture in your mind, use all your senses to make the visualization as real as possible. Imagine what it would look like, sound like, feel like, and even smell like. Allow yourself to fully immerse in this mental image and notice how it makes you feel.

Stay with this visualization for as long as you'd like, and allow yourself to feel the emotions that come with it. If your mind starts to wander, gently bring your focus back to your mental image and continue with the practice.

As you practice visualization meditation regularly, you'll begin to notice a shift in your energy and a greater sense of alignment with your desires. You'll start to attract opportunities and experiences that are in alignment with your vision, and you'll feel more confident and empowered to create the life you want.

* * *

Quote of the day:

"Imagination is everything. It is the preview of life's coming attractions." – Albert Einstein.

Food for thought:
What is one thing you've always wanted to experience, but have been too afraid to pursue? How can visualization meditation help you overcome your fears and manifest your desires?

Journal line:
Today, I visualized my dream scenario and felt the emotions that came with it. I am excited to see how this practice will impact my life in the future.

_____

_____

_____
_____
_____
_____
_____
_____

WELCOME TO THE FINAL DAY OF OUR 7-DAY MEDITATION CHALLENGE!

We hope that you've enjoyed this journey so far and have found value in each of the meditations we've explored together. For our last day, we will be practicing a silent meditation.

Silent meditation is a powerful tool to connect with your inner self and cultivate a sense of stillness and calmness within. It allows you to observe your thoughts without getting caught up in them, and to simply be in the present moment.

To begin, find a comfortable and quiet place to sit. Close your eyes and take a few deep breaths to center yourself. Allow your breath to become natural and focus on the sensation of air moving in and out of your body.

As you continue to breathe, allow your thoughts to come and go without getting attached to them. Simply observe them from a distance, like watching clouds passing by in the sky.

If you find your mind wandering, gently bring your attention back to your breath. You may find it helpful to count your breaths or repeat a mantra to help anchor your focus.

Practice this meditation for at least 10 minutes or longer if you feel comfortable. When you're ready, slowly open your eyes and take a moment to appreciate the stillness and calmness you've created within yourself.

Quote for the day:

"Silence is a source of great strength." - Lao Tzu.

Food for thought:
What did you learn about yourself during this meditation challenge? What insights did you gain about your inner world?

Journal line:
Take a few minutes to reflect on your experience with the 7-day meditation challenge. How did it impact you? What changes did you notice in your mental and emotional state? What new habits will you continue to cultivate moving forward?

_____
_____
_____
_____
_____
_____
_____
_____

_____
_____
_____
_____
_____
_____
_____
_____

CONGRATULATIONS, YOU'VE COMPLETED THE 7-DAY MEDITATION CHALLENGE!

Through this journey, you've explored various meditation practices that have helped you deepen your connection with your inner self and cultivate a sense of inner peace. You've learned to be present in the moment, to observe your thoughts and emotions without judgment, to cultivate compassion, gratitude, and forgiveness, and to visualize your dreams into reality.

Meditation is a powerful tool that can transform your life. By taking the time to quiet your mind, you can tap into your intuition, find clarity, and gain a new perspective on life. It's a practice that can help you stay centered amidst the chaos of daily life and develop a greater sense of self-awareness.

But don't stop here! Make meditation a regular part of your life. Commit to taking at least a few minutes every day to sit in silence, breathe deeply, and connect with your inner self. You'll be amazed at how this simple practice can bring more peace, joy, and clarity into your life.

. . .

Remember, as the Zen proverb goes, "You should sit in meditation for twenty minutes every day—unless you're too busy. Then you should sit for an hour." So, even if you're busy, take a moment to meditate. It's a gift to yourself that keeps on giving.

Thank you for taking this journey with me. I hope that you continue to explore the world of meditation and find the peace and clarity you seek. Namaste.

Personal notes:

* * *

- _____
- _____
- _____
- _____
- _____
- _____
- _____
- _____
- _____
- _____
- _____
- _____
- _____
- _____
- _____
- _____
- _____

Resources

Ramos, B. P. (2019). *The Art of Stress-Free Living: Reprogram Your Life From the Inside Out.* Morgan James Publishing.

* * *

Van Der Kolk, B. A. (2015). *The Body Keeps the Score: Brain, Mind, and Body in the Healing of Trauma.* Penguin Books.

* * *

McMillen, K., & McMillen, A. (2001). *When I Loved Myself Enough.* Macmillan.

* * *

Scott, L. (2003). *Sober Kitchen: Recipes and Advice for a Lifetime of Sobriety.* Harvard Common Press.

***

Balmer, R. H. (2004). *Encyclopedia of Evangelicalism*. Baylor University Press.

***

Feynman, R. P. (2015). *The Quotable Feynman*. Princeton University Press.

***

Hanh, T. N. (2015). The Miracle of Mindfulness. *Accommodation and Acceptance*, 221–238. https://doi.org/10.2307/j.ctt19705fq.15

***

Rosch, E. (2007). More Than Mindfulness: When You Have a Tiger by the Tail, Let It Eat You. *Psychological Inquiry*, 18(4), 258–264. https://doi.org/10.1080/10478400701598371

***

Cheung, T. (2020). *100 Ways to Be Kind: Everyday Actions to Change Your Life and Save the World*. Thread.

***

Mulcahy, S. (2016). *Reflections of the Heart*. Balboa Press.

***

Regan, L. (2020). *Quotes by Albert Einstein: The Complete Collection of Over 150 Quotes*. Independently Published.

* * *

Yip, K. (2005). Taoistic concepts of mental health: Implications for social work practice with Chinese communities. *Families in society-The Journal of Contemporary Social Services*. https://doi.org/10.1606/1044-3894.1875

Afterword

* * *

In conclusion, meditation is a powerful tool for women to connect with their inner selves and find peace, balance, and joy in their lives. By exploring various meditation practices, such as mindfulness, body scan, loving-kindness, gratitude, forgiveness, visualization, and silent meditation, women can deepen their connection with their inner wisdom, enhance their emotional well-being, and improve their overall health and quality of life. Whether you are new to meditation or an experienced practitioner, there is always something new to discover and explore. Remember to be patient and compassionate with yourself and to make meditation a regular part of your self-care routine. May these meditations serve as a guide and inspiration on your journey toward inner peace and well-being.

Epilogue

As you reach the end of "The Best Meditations for Women," take a moment to reflect on the journey you have taken. You have explored daily meditations designed to help you connect with your inner wisdom, intuition, and creativity. You have learned how to cultivate a greater sense of self-awareness and self-love, which are essential components of living a fulfilling and meaningful life.

By practicing these meditations, you have discovered how to calm your mind, reduce stress, improve your focus, and enhance your overall well-being. You have taken small steps each day to tap into your inner strength and wisdom, allowing you to navigate life's challenges with greater ease and grace.

The quotes and food for thought throughout the book have inspired and uplifted you, giving you new perspectives on life and yourself. Writing in your journal has allowed you to deepen your connection with yourself and your inner wisdom, providing you with valuable insights and reflections.

. . .

As you continue to practice these meditations, you will notice a profound shift in your energy and perspective. You will feel more centered and grounded, more connected to your inner self and the world around you. Your stress levels will decrease, your focus will improve, and your overall sense of well-being will be enhanced.

I hope this book has served as a valuable tool on your journey toward greater well-being, joy, and fulfillment. Remember, meditation is a practice that you can continue to cultivate throughout your life, and the benefits are endless.

Thank you for taking the time to explore "The Best Meditations for Women." I am honored to have been a part of your journey toward inner peace and strength.

About the Author

Bio

Meet me, a passionate and multi-talented individual with a deep love for life and learning. I have always been driven by my desire to explore new horizons and develop my skills.

One of my greatest passions is photography. I find joy in capturing beautiful moments and preserving memories for a lifetime. Whether it's experimenting with new techniques or taking stunning landscape shots, I am always looking to push myself and expand my capabilities.

In addition to photography, I am also an avid artist and teacher. I enjoy using my creativity to inspire others and help them explore their own artistic talents. As a life coach and spiritual guide, I am dedicated to helping people find their inner peace and achieve their personal goals.

As an essential oil advocate, I am passionate about natural health and wellness. I believe in the power of aromatherapy and love sharing my knowledge and experience with others.

In all of my endeavors, I am driven by my passion for life and my desire to make a positive impact on the world around me. Whether through my art, my teachings, or my work, I am constantly seeking new ways to grow and evolve as a person.

I am a highly enthusiastic and self-motivated individual with a diverse set of skills and experiences. With over 15 years of military service, I have developed a solid foundation of discipline, leadership, and determination.

In addition to my military experience, I have over 10 years of experience in the retail and wholesale business. My passion for customer service and satisfaction has led to a successful track record in achieving sales goals and building strong relationships with clients.

For over 11 years, I have also been involved in the school environment, taking on leadership roles in the community. I have organized and led teams of students and parents in various initiatives such as fundraisers, teaching, volunteering, and more. My ability to inspire and motivate others has been a key factor in the success of these efforts.

In addition to my leadership skills, I also have experience in event organization, public speaking, and volunteering. As an art instructor, I have had the opportunity to share my creativity and passion for the arts.

Currently, I am in the process of writing my own books, where I plan to share all my experiences and insights gained throughout my career. I am excited to inspire and motivate others through my writing and continue to make a positive impact on the world around me.

CoreSpirit
Twitter
Facebook
Medium
Amazon

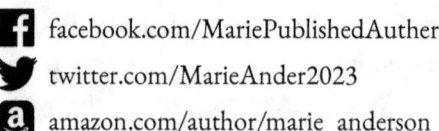

facebook.com/MariePublishedAuther
twitter.com/MarieAnder2023
amazon.com/author/marie_anderson

www.ingramcontent.com/pod-product-compliance
Lightning Source LLC
Chambersburg PA
CBHW071033080526
44587CB00015B/2597